W9-AVK-255

This Diary is

mine!

And this is Me!

♡ Sign here.

My ideas need expressing*

* All of the wild and crazy expressions in this book
are the private property of ME!

ABOUT THE AUTHOR

that's me!

Real name

Nickname

Secret identity

Stage name

Royal name

Age

I was born (city)   (state)

My email address is

Date I started this book

Date completed

This is **NOT** just another diary!

Oh No!!

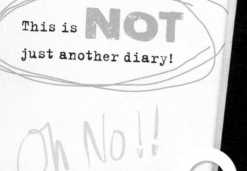

♥ Place your ♥ photo here

ILLUSTRATION/DESIGN BY NANCY PANACCIONE

Fine Print Publishing Company
P.O. Box 916401
Longwood, FL 32791-6401

ISBN 978-189295167-0

Copyright © 2013 by Nancy Panaccione

All rights reserved worldwide. No part of this work may be
reproduced or transmitted or stored in any form by any means,
electronic or mechanical, including photocopy, recording,
information storage and retrieval system, or otherwise, without
permission in writing from the publisher.

This book is printed on acid-free paper.

Created in the U.S.A. & Printed in China

10 9

(OKay...) this is a warm-up page.
Use it to try out different pencils and pens
to find your favorite. Then ...

On my mind today ...

EXPRESS YOURSELF
AND CLICK IT CLOSED!

Try Drawing something.

My eye color ● ● ● ⊙

My hair color ● ● ⊙ ⊙ ● ● ○ (hair color not here? add it)

I am the (⊙ only ● youngest ● middle ⊙ oldest) child

The song playing right now is

_____

My best friend is

R o b y

I live with

(⊙ both parents ● one parent

● grandparents ⊙ siblings ● another guardian)

I love to

_____

_____

_____

I stay in touch with my friends by

● texting them ⊙ calling from my cell

● Leaving messages on Facebook

● Seeing them at my activities

● Seeing them at school

I'm fabulous because

I would love to travel to ⤳

My pets

Height ↕   Weight ↔
My lucky number   The Grade I'm in

What I ate today

What I'm wearing right now

The time I go to bed

Most fun thing I did today

One thing I can't live without

The thing I would (LOVE) to change about my world

My Faves

TV shows

Song

Movie

Book

Store

Mall

Actor/Actress

Singer

Band

Board game

Magazine

City

Food/Snack

Ice cream flavor

Pizza topping

Vegetable

Fruit

and Raves

Restaurant

Color

Animal

School Subject

Teacher

Gadget

Room in the house

Month of the year

Season

Cartoon character

Halloween costume

Stuffed animal

Social Media (pick one or more)

○ Twitter   ○ Instagram   ○ Pinterest

○ Tumblr   ○ Facebook   ○ (Other)

Here's the real deal on Me & My Friends.

Friends Til the End

Draw or paste a funny photo of your friends, or just doodle their names in the photo boxes.

Name

But I call him or her

ONE word to describe my friend

....

.... is totally cool because

....

....

ONE word to describe my friend

....

.... is totally cool because

....

....

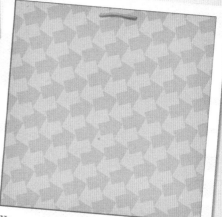

Name

But I call him or her

Name

But I call him or her

ONE word to describe my friend

....

.... is totally cool because

....

....

ONE word to describe my friend

....

.... is totally cool because

....

....

Name
But I call him or her

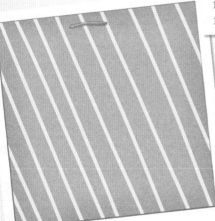

Name
But I call him or her

ONE word to describe my friend

....

.... is totally cool because

....

....

ONE word to describe my friend

....

.... is totally cool because

....

....

Name
But I call him or her

ONE word to describe my friend

....

.... is totally cool because

....

....

Name

But I call him or her

ONE word to describe my friend

....

.... is totally cool because

....

....

Name

But I call him or her

Name

But I call him or her

ONE word to describe my friend

....

.... is totally cool because

....

....

My Busy Life

WRITE A STORY ABOUT YOUR CRAZY LIFE

IT ALL STARTED WHEN...

My Story

once lived a Girl named Tess. she was a good girl but one day she had to oo to school. When tess went to school she had no freinds. but it seemed like everyone else had freinds. When tess tried to make freinds she couldn't. But one day a little girl cam up to her and said do you want to be freinds Tess was a litte shy but she said yes her cheeks were turni red. as she played with th little girl. Tess wonderd what her name was. one duy tess went up to her and said what your name. she said maya.

and I'm stickin' to it
author: me   illaustrator: me

The end.

Oh Yeah!

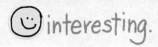 interesting.

After school, I _____

_____

I have after-school chores "Oh yeah!" or "No way!"

If yes, my chores are _____

My BFF's and I can talk for hours about _____

_____

After school, ○ I start my homework immediately
               ○ I watch TV and then do my homework

My favorite thing to do on the weekend is _____

_____

MY FRIENDS AND I L♥VE TO GO:

○ To the Mall   ○ To the Park   ○ To Dance   ○ To Soccer

TRANSPORTATION:

○ A parent drives me where I want to go.   ○ I walk.
○ I take the bus.   ○ I ride my bike or board.

When we're together, my friends and I . . .

Switch your pen or pencil to the hand that you don't normally write with.

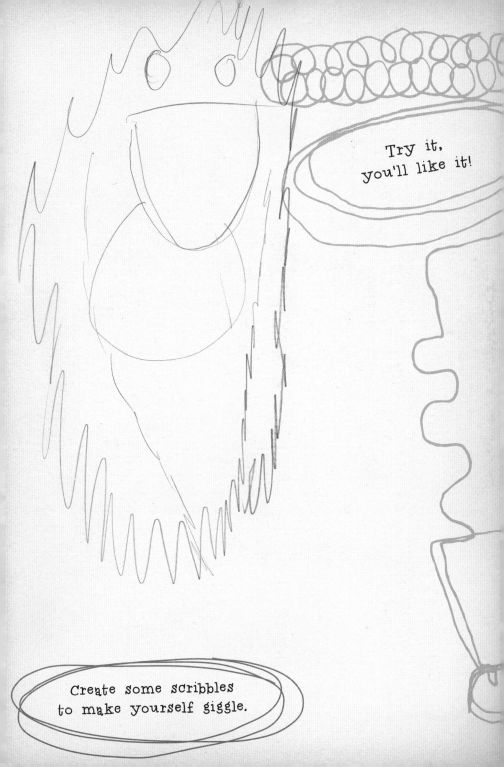

Try it,
you'll like it!

Create some scribbles
to make yourself giggle.

Try closing your eyes
while you draw.

Dearest diary, im
having a pretty bad day
first I got blamed for
hurting my sister and then
my mom got mad at
me because she thought
I was being mean to
my sister and my
friend was being a little
mean too I ll give you a list
she pushed me on the
stairs she choked me and
she pushed me, there
you have it.

Do your scribbles look like
anything? Write about what
they remind you of.

Awesome

some

APPLICATION FOR A COMPLAINT

TO BE COMPLETED BY THE COMPLAINER (Please Print):

Section 1

Instructions:

1. Attach a photo of yourself to this form, in the box to the right. Make sure you have your complaining face on.

2. Fill out, sign, and date this form.

3. In order to process this form, you must show it to your best friend.

(Please note: InKoreckt speling voids this complaint.)
If complaint doesn't fit in the space alloted, too bad.

> AFFIX
> complainer's
> photo here.

Section 2

Complainer's Name

Elliz

Address

100 North park Ave.

Birthday   Email address

sept. 20

Please **CIRCLE** day of the week incident occurred: M   T   W   (Th)   F   S   S

Section 3

Please state who this complaint is against.   Me

Please state reason for complaining.   She thought I was hurting her.

When was the last time you filled out a complaint form? For what complaint?   Never

_____   _maddie_____
Date   Signature

OFFICE COPY   Form#5986NH87469201

Turn the page to continue complaining...

APPLICATION FOR A COMPLAINT

APPLICATION FOR A COMPLAINT

TO BE COMPLETED BY THE COMPLAINER (Please Print):

Section 1

Instructions:

1. Attach a photo of yourself to this form, in the box to the right. Make sure you have your complaining face on.

2. Fill out, sign, and date this form.

3. In order to process this form, you must show it to your best friend.

(Please note: InKoreckt speling voids this complaint.)
If complaint doesn't fit in the space alloted, too bad.

> **AFFIX**
> **complainer's**
> **photo here.**

Section 2

_____
Complainer's Name

_____
Address

_____
Birthday   Email address

Please **CIRCLE** day of the week incident occurred: M   T   W   Th   F   S   S

Section 3

Please state who this complaint is against. _____

Please state reason for complaining. _____

_____

_____

_____

When was the last time you filled out a complaint form? For what complaint? _____

_____

_____

_____   _____
Date   Signature

OFFICE COPY   Form#5986NH87469201

APPLICATION FOR A COMPLAINT

TO BE COMPLETED BY THE COMPLAINER (Please Print):

Section 1

Instructions:

1. Attach a photo of yourself to this form, in the box to the right.
   Make sure you have your complaining face on.

2. Fill out, sign, and date this form.

3. In order to process this form, you must show it to
   your best friend.

(Please note: InKoreckt speling voids this complaint.)
If complaint doesn't fit in the space alloted, too bad.

> **AFFIX**
> complainer's
> photo here.

Section 2

_____

Complainer's Name

_____

Address

_____

Birthday   Email address

Please **CIRCLE** day of the week incident occurred: M   T   W   Th   F   S   S

Section 3

Please state who this complaint is against. _____

Please state reason for complaining. _____

_____

_____

_____

When was the last time you filled out a complaint form? For what complaint? _____

_____

_____

_____   _____
Date   Signature

OFFICE COPY   Form#5986NH87469201

me   sister   brother

mom

DaD

Here's my family and they rock . . .

sometimes!

Draw or paste a funny
photo of your family
members on these pages.

Don't forget to add
funny captions!

What's Your Name?

WRITE YOUR
FIRST AND LAST NAME
IN THE BOXES
PROVIDED, BUT
YOU HAVE TO
WRITE IT LIKE
IT SAYS.

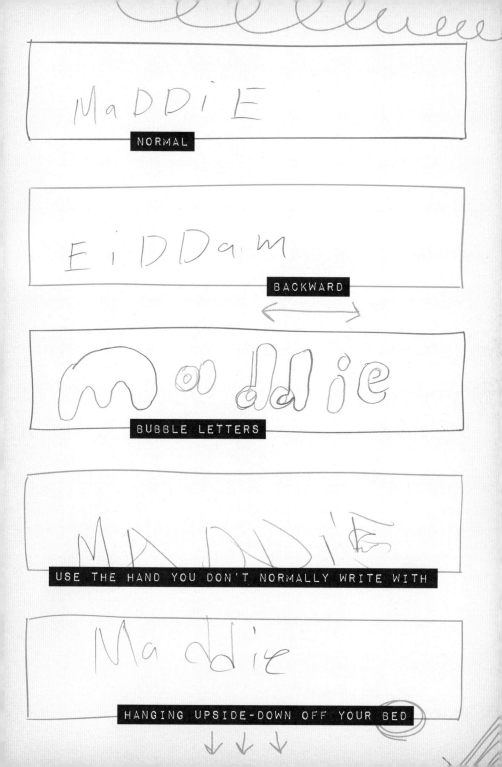

MaDDiE

NORMAL

EiDDam

BACKWARD

moddie

BUBBLE LETTERS

MADDiE

USE THE HAND YOU DON'T NORMALLY WRITE WITH

Maddie

HANGING UPSIDE-DOWN OFF YOUR BED

Maddie

WITH YOUR EYES CLOSED

IN LIPSTICK

Maddie

WITHOUT LIFTING YOUR PEN OR PENCIL FROM THE BOOK

MADDIE

LOOKING IN THE MIRROR

MADDIE

BEHIND YOUR BACK

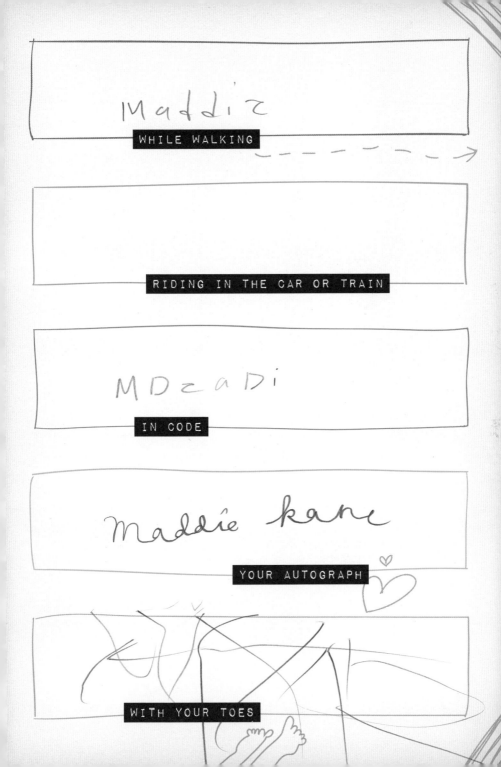

Maddic

WHILE WALKING

RIDING IN THE CAR OR TRAIN

MDzaDi

IN CODE

maddie kane

YOUR AUTOGRAPH

WITH YOUR TOES

Or deny authority and add graffiti all over them.

Are You
expressing
Yourself?

Don't worry! This book is all locked up.

HI

Write some secret TRUTHS about YOU that NO ONE knows.

TRUTH

#1 I said 'I love you to a man.

#2 pead pants

#3 scream pillows

#4 sleep stuffed animals

#5

#6

#7

#8

Hey! What would you like people to know?

_____
_____
_____
_____
_____
_____
_____
_____
_____
_____
_____
_____
_____
_____
_____
_____
_____

Are your ideas
expressed and
locked?

Denim
Doodles FINE!

NOT allowed to write on your jeans?

You can doodle all over these jeans.
Use gel pens, different colors, or glue stuff down.

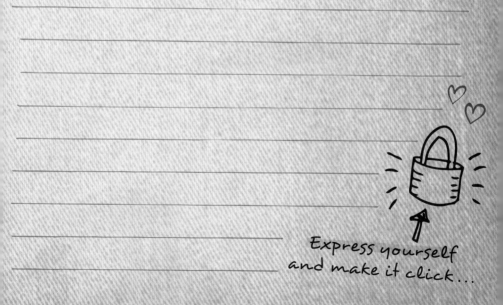

Express yourself
and make it click...

I was thinking may be
somehow I could make
a machine that could
dig up very fragile thing
like a big Dinosaur. or a
machine that can sens-
Trash. and it will pick it
up.

My Ideas Need expressing

My PERFECT Day!

Fill in the timeline of what you would do on the most wonderful day in the world!

6:00 am Sleeping

7:00 am get dressed

8:00 am getting ready for school

9:00 am doing school

10:00 am schco

11:00 am lunch

noon lunch   Mmmmm...

1:00 pm P.e. Music or Art

2:00 pm math

3:00 pm done with school

4:00 pm play outside

5:00 pm diner

6:00 pm Movie

7:00 pm bed

8:00 pm Sleep / watcha show

9:00 pm Sleeping

z z z z
10:00 pm Sleep dreaming

11:00 pm No

Are you
still up?

Daydream some more

about your perfect day. Write down all of the juicy details.

_____
_____
_____
_____
_____
_____
_____
_____
_____
_____
_____
_____
_____
_____
_____
_____
_____
_____
_____
_____

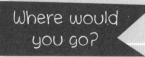

Where would
you go?

_____
_____

DREAM

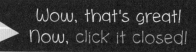
Wow, that's great!
Now, click it closed!

The Bucket

1.
2.
3.
4.
5.
6.
7.
8.
9.
10.
11.
12.
13.
14.
15.
16.
17.
18.
19.
20.
21.
22.

List

Write a list of wild and crazy things that you want to do in your life.

23.

24.

25.

26.

27.

28.

29.

30.

31.

32.

33.

34.

35.

36.

37.

38.

39.

40.

41.

42.

43.

44.

A STICKY Situation

Whones I put so much
glue on a pregect that
my fingers got stuck
to / gether

STICK it down!

my dream is
to/be the first
women on the mens leag.

You know the drill.
CLICK it closed!

TRUTH

Tell the truth and nothing but the truth!

If you found a wallet full of money, would you return it? (Yes or No)
Why? _____
_____
_____
_____

If your best friend hurt you, you would... _____
_____
_____
_____

If you could read a friend's diary, would you? (Yes or No)
Why? _____
_____
_____

If you could trade places with anyone in the world, it would be...
_____
Why? _____
_____

Telling the truth can be tough.

Write about a time where you had to tell a difficult truth.

_____

_____

_____

_____

_____

_____

_____

_____

_____

_____

_____

_____

_____

_____

_____

_____

_____

_____

DARE

Do each thing on this list
for a whole day.

Check them off
as you do them.

Wear your shirt inside-out. ○

Sing out loud on your way to class. ○

Take photos of a friend without her knowing. ○

Say "Yes, or No, Ma'am" or "Yes, or No, Sir," to everyone today. ○

Wear different types of socks, make sure they show. ○

Talk with an accent. ○

Don't use your thumbs. ○

Don't use technology, NO computers, phones, TVs, MP3s, etc. ○

Wear a superhero cape at school. ○

Wear an outfit that totally clashes. ○

Give a piggyback ride to one of your friends. ○

Attach toilet paper to your shoe and walk around with it. ○

Hold onto a friend's shoulder and have them lead you around. ○

Tell everyone where you are ticklish. ○

Talk like a cartoon character. ○

So how did your DARE go?
Write down all of the fun details.

_____

_____

_____

_____

_____

_____

_____

_____

_____

_____

_____

_____

_____

_____

_____

_____

_____

It's all you

Express
Yourself

Here's your chance!

Be BOLD or close this book!

Write it down or scribble it out.

Express it
& click it!

DESIGN A WORD

Color in these words, and then create your own words to decorate.

Awesome

LUV

L8R

LOL

Crazy

WOW!

KABOOM!

COOL

the
Escape
Hatch

This is a doorway
to another dimension.

Where are you going?
What does it look like?
Tell the story.

THAT SMELL

Take this book to a department store. Spray one of the clouds with your favorite perfume. Every time you go back, try a different perfume in another cloud.

The perfume will make this whole book smell good!

make sure
you label your
FAVES
to remember
for l8ter.

How I would describe my **appearance** _____

_____

_____

My _____ is my best feature.

I look *fabulous* when I wear _____

I feel very comfortable wearing _____

How I take care of me _____

_____

_____

A clothing trend that I like_____

A clothing trend that I don't like _____

I eat Healthy or Junk Food (circle one)

Here's how I *chill* _____

_____

_____

My **favorite** piece of jewelry is _____

My **favorite** shoes are _____

My **favorite** piece of clothing is _____

The color that looks fab on me is _____

My *favorite exercise* is_____

I exercise

○ once a week   ○ twice a week   ○ when my friends do ○ NEVER!

Cut out pictures of your favorite shoes and glue or tape them on the shoe racks.

I would describe my fashion Style as...

_____
_____
_____
_____
_____
_____
_____
_____
_____
_____
_____
_____
_____
_____

Do designer labels matter to you?

_____
_____

my FAVE
accessory is...
_____

fashion

My Go-To
outfit is...

My style is unique!

Draw your most awesome DREAM outfit here.

My FAVE
piece of jewelry

The BEST
perfume ever!

My FAVE
brand of jeans

The ONLY
backpack I will carry

OPEN the VENT!

➡️ Complain, grumble, and whine ⬅️
all about the things that get
on your nerves and annoy you.

Parent on your case?

Crummy Day?

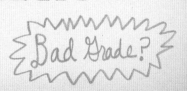

Bad Grade?

{you and your best friend have a blow up?}

_____

_____

_____

_____

_____

_____

_____

_____

_____

_____

_____

_____

_____

_____

_____

_____

_____

_____

_____

_____

_____

Whine, scream, and carry on!

Now that you let it out,
don't forget to "click it closed!"

Have you "HERD"?

Use these pages to write down all of the juicy gossip and secrets you're keeping. Don't forget to click it closed!

"Holy Cow."

Would you star in your movie?

Location?

Genre? ○ action/adventure ○ comedy ○ romance
○ sci-fi ○ thriller ○ mystery

Actors/Actresses?

Hero/Heroine?

Happy ending or sad ending?

Scene 1:

Scene 2:

Scene 3:

♥ THE END?

Write down a time that you were stunned, shocked, or wowed.

I lahge so hard.
that I can,t breth. I like
drama. and I get
in banissed infront
of my friene.
Sometimes I note
name where you rite
Your name

Creative GENIUS STRIKES!

That's YOU!

You only have 1 minute to scribble it down, color it up, or glue, glue, glue! GO!

Come back later
and try again
on the next page!

Draw something special
in this circle.

What's all the
Stink about?

HaHa
HaHaHa

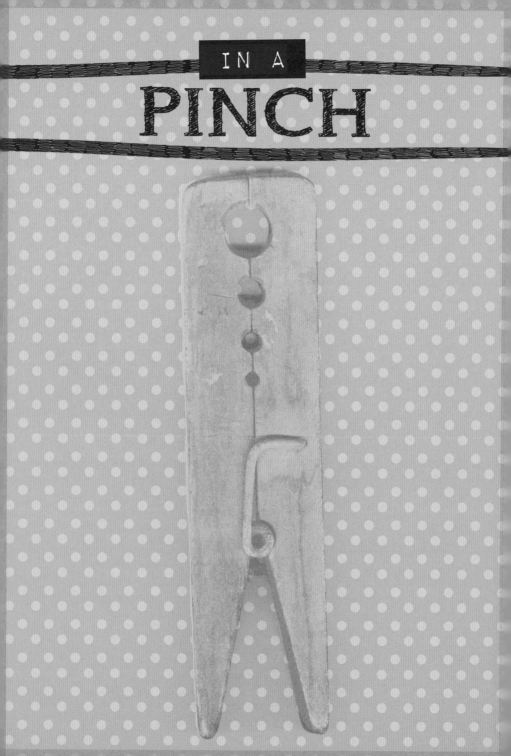

IN A

PINCH

WRITE DOWN A TIME YOU WERE
CAUGHT IN A PINCH AND HOW YOU GOT OUT OF IT

Will you ever
get stuck in a
pinch again?

WHEN LIFE GIVES YOU
LEMONS...

DID IT RAIN ON YOU TODAY?

DID YOU GET SPLASHED WITH MUD?

DID YOU LOSE YOUR FAVORITE SWEATER?

WRITE DOWN EVERYTHING THAT MAKES YOU SAD, ANGRY, OR AFRAID.

THE SKY
IS FALLING!

THE SKY
IS FALLING!

Sunshine & Lollipops

Write down the best way for you to feel happy, joyful, and smiley!

The world is full
of rainbows.

This is my

SECRET

hiding place.

GLue

a real envelope to this page.
Hide your best ideas inside.

QUICK!
Click this
book closed!!!

click

THIS DIARY WAS
COMPLETED ON:

/ /

I did it!